CONTENTS

STEP INTO THE WORLD OF
ANCIENT
ROME

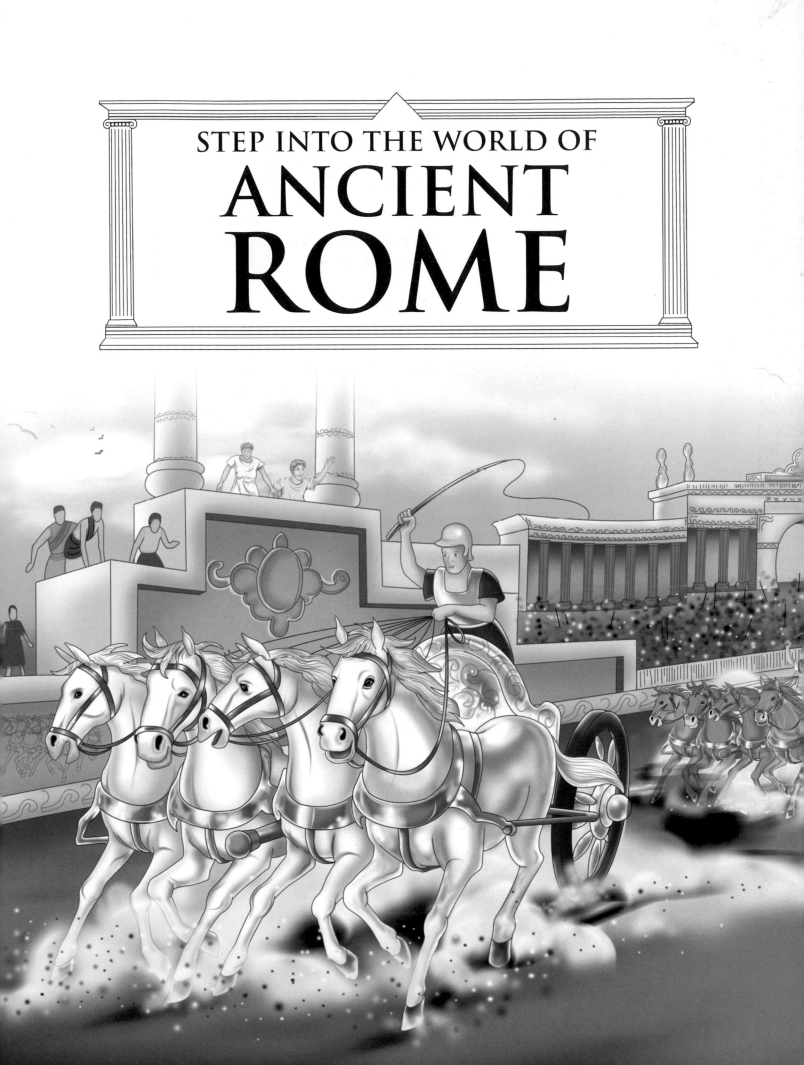

CONTENTS

RULERS

The history of the early Roman kings is a mixture of legends and facts. There were great rulers like Augustus and Hadrian.

The First Kings

Tarquinius Priscus improved Rome by draining the marshes there and building a temple for the Roman god Jupiter. Servius Tullius is said to have built a wall around the seven hills on which Rome was situated.

A wreath of laurel leaves was a symbol of power and influence

Later, Rome became a republic ruled by representatives from the senate (a council of noblemen). The letters SPQR ("the senate and the people of Rome") were often engraved on items such as shields and coins.

Rulers of the Republic

Augustus was the first of the emperors recognised by the senate. Romulus Augustus was the last emperor of the Roman Empire in Europe. The emperors wore a laurel wreath as a symbol of their authority.

The letters SPQR represented the status of Rome as a republic

What does the saying "Nero fiddled while Rome burned" refer to?

In A.D. 64, during the reign of the emperor Nero, the city of Rome was destroyed by a massive fire. The saying "Nero fiddled while Rome burned" refers to the popular legend that the infamous, mad emperor played his lyre and sang while he watched Rome burn!

Nobody knows whether Nero really played his "fiddle" (lyre) while Rome was burning!

 Which Roman emperor changed his name to Augustus?

Julius Caesar's nephew, Octavian, changed his name to Augustus and established himself as the first Roman emperor in 27 B.C.

Who was the first Roman emperor to sport a beard?

Hadrian was known to be the first Roman emperor to wear a full beard!

A special "crocodile coin" was issued to celebrate Rome's conquest of Egypt

Which ancient Roman king was overthrown so that Rome could become a republic?

In 509 B.C., the unjust king Tarquinius Superbus was driven out of Rome by a group of Roman noblemen. In the absence of a ruler, Rome became a republic.

When did Emperor Augustus issue a special coin?

Emperor Augustus issued a special coin after his conquest of Egypt. The coin had an image of a crocodile.

Julius Caesar was stabbed to death by his own senators

Who is considered to be one of the greatest ancient Roman leaders although he never became emperor?

Julius Caesar was a very powerful military general and considered to be one of the greatest leaders of ancient Rome. He was not an emperor because Rome was a republic at the time of his rule. In 44 B.C. he was murdered by his own senators, who felt he had become too powerful and was likely to crown himself as emperor.

Which Roman emperor divided the empire into two parts?

Emperor Diocletian divided the Roman Empire into two. After that, there was one ruler for the west and another for the east.

■ In A.D. 330, the Roman emperor Constantine founded a new capital for his empire and named it Constantinople. This city of Constantinople, now called Istanbul, is one of the most historic cities in modern Turkey.

■ When Emperor Vespasian began the construction of the Colosseum, it was called the Flavian amphitheatre. His sons, Domitian and Titus, later completed the structure in A.D. 80.

■ Emperor Caligula's name translates into "little boots". As a little boy, he used to dress up in military clothes and thus got the nickname from his father's soldiers.

A Roman soldier's sandal-type shoes were called "caligulae"

RULERS

 Who was Empress Theodora?

Empress Theodora was the wife of the Roman emperor Justinian I. She ruled as an equal by his side and is thought to have been beautiful, intelligent and a very able ruler. There is a vivid portrait of her in the famous mosaic of Ravenna.

 Which city did the emperor Constantine rename in his own honour?

The emperor Constantine renamed the city of Byzantine in his own honour and called it Constantinople.

 Which ruler changed the Roman calendar?

The ancient Roman calendar had only 355 days to a year. Later, Julius Caesar added 10 more days to increase it to 365 .

The romantic story of Antony and Cleopatra captured Shakespeare's imagination

Which statue did Emperor Nero supposedly imitate when he had his own statue made?

Emperor Nero's huge statue of himself was probably an imitation of the massive ancient Greek statue, Colossus of Rhodes, which was one of the Seven Wonders of the Ancient World.

 Which plays by William Shakespeare are based on Roman leaders?

Shakespeare's play *Julius Caesar* is based on the life of the great Roman leader. In *Antony and Cleopatra*, Shakespeare explores the life of Mark Antony (Marcus Antonius), a leader of the Eastern Roman Empire, and his relationship with Cleopatra, the Egyptian queen.

PEOPLE

The Roman people were ordered into various ranks, which were given great importance.

Role of women

Rich women usually stayed indoors so they could complete the household chores and also watch the children. Poor women worked everyday in the houses and fields.

Romans were fond of good food and lavish feasts

Leisure

Roman citizens had a lot of time for leisure. Men visited the forum and relaxed at the bathhouses.

Food

The rich gave huge dinner parties, where diners were served meat, fish and fruits by slaves. Honey was used to sweeten the food. Poor people ate bean soup and bread.

Education

Roman students were taught to become effective speakers. The school day began before sunrise, and students had to bring candles with them! Girls learnt to spin, weave and sew at home.

PEOPLE

 What was a toga?

In ancient Rome, both men and women wore a knee-length gown called a tunic. The men draped a garment called toga over their tunic. Stripes or borders on the toga indicated the rank and position of the wearer.

A married Roman woman wore a stola over her tunic

An upper-class Roman man wore a toga over his tunic

 What did women in ancient Rome wear over the tunic?

Women in ancient Rome wore the stola over the tunic. The stola was a long garment, held with a belt around the waist.

What was the "lararium" in a Roman home?

Ancient Roman homes usually had a shrine called the "lararium", which served as a place of worship. Libations (liquids) such as milk, oil and wine were poured over the sacrificial fire lit on the altar.

What was the sarcophagus (flesh eater in Greek) that the ancient Romans used?

The ancient Romans buried their dead in a carved marble coffin known as a sarcophagus.

10

Why did Roman men wear signet rings?

Signet rings were used as seals to stamp important documents. A Roman man would press his signet ring on hot sealing wax to display his stamp of authority.

Signet ring

Why did the ancient Romans visit bathhouses?

The ancient Roman baths were places where people met their friends, and even conducted business. Apart from taking a bath at the bathhouses, they also exercised and swam.

Did Roman children play with bones?

Roman children played knuckle bones, a game of dice, by using dried sheep bones called *astragali*.

Children play a popular game with dried sheep's bones

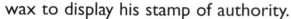

FACT BOX

■ There were educated slaves in ancient Rome. Known as "pedagogues", they taught the children of rich Romans.

■ Young men in ancient Rome went to schools of rhetoric in order to learn public speaking, or oratory. The study of rhetoric prepared them for careers in law and government. They could expertly debate various topics in the Roman Senate.

■ Ancient Romans used a pointed tool called stylus for "writing" on wax-coated boards. They scratched letters on these boards with the sharp tip of the stylus.

The stylus was a writing tool with a sharp tip

PEOPLE

A gold bracelet in the shape of a coiled snake

 Which reptile was featured on Roman jewellery?

In ancient Rome both men and women were fond of wearing jewellery. One type of bracelet, in the shape of a coiled snake, was very fashionable.

 What were the two basic types of tunic worn by Roman women?

Roman women's tunic (tunica) were made in two basic styles - the chiton and the peplos. Compared to the similar garb worn by Roman men, the women's tunic was fuller and longer, usually extending to the feet.

 Who were the four types of gladiators?

There were four main categories of gladiators, who were distinguished by the kind of armour they wore, the weapons they used, and their style of fighting. They were called Thracian, Secutor, Retiarius and Bestiarius.

 How did Roman clothes show the status of the wearer?

The type of clothes that a Roman person wore indicated his or her place in society. A citizen would wear a toga and a married woman would usually wear a stola. A senator sported coloured shoes and displayed a wide stripe on his toga. People from the lower classes wore gathered-up tunics.

Romans made sure they were well-groomed!

 Did ancient Romans use tweezers?

The ancient Romans used plenty of grooming aids to make themselves look better. They had tweezers for plucking out hair, fine combs, decorative hairpins and even small scoopers to remove earwax.

GAMES AND ENTERTAINMENT

Ancient Romans enjoyed lots of games and entertainments. Poor people, too, could attend most events because these were free. Even the smallest of the large open-air theatres had space for up to 7,000 people.

Wild Contests

Romans went to the Colosseum to watch gladiator fights and contests between wild animals and men. Sometimes the Colosseum was filled with water for staging of naval battles!

Speedy Steeds

At the Circus Maximus, up to 250,000 spectators could watch thrilling chariot races. Other smaller circuses (open-air stadiums) regularly held events.

They Had a Ball!

The Romans indulged in various activities - from riding, fencing and hunting to ball games like soccer, trigon and harpastum. While trigon was played with a hard ball, harpastum used a small ball. The ancient Romans, in fact, were the first to introduce soccer in Britain!

Ball games were very popular in ancient Rome

GAMES AND ENTERTAINMENT

 **What was a hippodrome?**

In ancient Rome, horse and chariot races took place at the hippodrome. Spectators sat on rows of tiered seats, while the racing track itself was divided into laps.

 Why was chariot racing a dangerous sport?

Chariot racing was both dangerous and exciting because the chariots, which were pulled by two or four horses, were driven at very high speeds. Accidents took place quite frequently and participants risked being crushed to death.

 Where did Roman men gather to exercise and play sports?

The Campus was an area in the city that had a track and field. Roman men gathered there to exercise and play sports. They engaged in activities such as boxing, wrestling, sprinting, jumping and archery.

 On what occasions could the ancient Romans gamble?

Ancients Romans were allowed to place bets only at chariot races or gladiatorial fights. Gambling on other occasions was illegal, but probably there were secret houses where men gambled with dice and coins.

The thrilling sport of chariot racing was enjoyed by the Romans

Gladiators fought in an arena and entertained thousands of spectators

Who were the gladiators?

Gladiators were fighters who took part in contests to entertain the Roman masses. They got their name from *gladius*, a short sword. They were nearly always slaves or criminals. All gladiators had to take a solemn oath that they were prepared to die.

When did Roman spectators give a "thumbs up" signal?

When Roman spectators wanted a gladiator to be spared from death, they gave a "thumbs up" signal.

Did the ancient Romans play ball games?

Ancient Romans played many different types of ball games. Field hockey, *espulsim ludere* (handball), trigon, harpastum and Roman Ball were popular. There were all kinds of balls, such as bouncing balls, hard balls and soft balls. Some balls were made of linen and wool.

FACT BOX

■ Gladiators were rewarded with coins when they performed well and the audience was pleased with them. An outstanding gladiator, who managed to survive many fights, was sometimes set free from slavery. He was given a bone tablet, with his name engraved on it.

MODERATVS

Bone tablet

■ During games, different kinds of animals were brought from far and wide to entertain the people. Lions, giraffes, zebras and even alligators were a part of the contests. Sometimes wild animals like lions were kept hungry to make them more ferocious.

■ The Retiarius gladiator wore only a loin cloth and carried a net with which he could snare his opponent.

GAMES AND ENTERTAINMENT

 Why was a handkerchief dropped at the start of a chariot race?

An official dropped a handkerchief to signal the start of a chariot race. Four teams - made up of blues, reds, whites and greens - competed against each other.

 Where were prisoners and wild animals kept before fights?

The arena, which was the actual place where fights took place, had a maze of cages and dungeons underneath. Wild animals and prisoners were kept locked up there before being released into the arena.

A bestiarius gladiator pitted against a fierce lion

 Who was a Bestiarius?

A Bestiarius was a gladiator who fought against ferocious beasts. Roman people loved to watch contests between gladiators and wild animals. A Bestiarius was usually armed only with a whip and a spear.

 What kind of board games did the Romans play?

The Romans played a board game that is believed to be similar to the modern game of draughts. They used glass and pottery counters, and the dice were usually made of bone.

 How did bears entertain the Romans?

The Romans enjoyed the sport of bear-baiting in which specially trained dogs were made to attack a chained bear.

A board game with counters made of glass

ARCHITECTURE AND MONUMENTS

By the 1st century AD Rome was one of the biggest cities in the world, with splendid public buildings like temples, stadiums and baths. Two of the grandest Roman monuments were the Colosseum and the Pantheon.

Architecture

The Romans were greatly influenced by the architecture of the Greeks. However, the Romans had an advantage because they had concrete. They also used terracotta, brick and stone. Marble was costly and used sparingly.

Housing

Wealthy Romans (patricians) lived in villas. These faced inwards onto an open space called an atrium, with arcades to provide shade from the mid-day sun. The walls of the villas were made of clay and limestone. The richest Romans had three villas - one in the city, one in the country and one by the sea! The poor man, or the plebeian, lived in crowded buildings called insulae. These were usually six storeys high. The buildings were poorly ventilated and badly built, often even without toilets or kitchens.

The Colosseum is an outstanding landmark of ancient Rome

ARCHITECTURE AND MONUMENTS

 How colossal was the Colosseum?

The Colosseum (from the Greek word *kolossos*, meaning "enormous statue") was a huge amphitheatre that could seat about 50,000 people. It had a height of 48 metres, a length of nearly 189 metres and a width of about 155 metres. There were as many as 80 entrances.

 Which ancient Roman structure in the United Kingdom is a World Heritage site?

Hadrian's Wall - which marked the northern limit of the Roman emperor Hadrian's kingdom - is a World Heritage site. It had a length of 80 Roman miles (equivalent to 117 modern kilometres).

 Why did Romans spend so much time in the bath?

Of all the leisure activities, bathing was the most important for the Romans. It was part of the daily routine for men of all classes. Baths were great places to relax and meet friends. Nearly all big cities had bathhouses with steam baths, both warm and cold swimming pools, sports facilities and massages.

 Did the ancient Romans build pyramids?

After Rome's conquest of Egypt, the tombs of several eminent Romans were built in the shape of pyramids. The pyramid of Caius Cestius is one of the few that have survived.

 What was the Roman Forum?

The Roman Forum (*Forum Romanum*) was an important town square and marketplace. It contained some of the oldest monuments. These included the Rostra (a platform for speeches) and several temples, arches and statues.

Roman baths were heated by hot air that flowed in through a space beneath the floor

The Pantheon is an example of Roman architecture at its best

 Which god was the Pantheon temple dedicated to?

The Pantheon was originally dedicated to not one, but to all the ancient Roman gods. We now use the word "pantheon" (which means "of all gods") to refer to a collection of gods. The Pantheon, which had the biggest dome of its time, was later used as a Catholic church.

Why did a Roman house have an atrium?

An atrium was a large, bright and airy room in a wealthy Roman's house. It had an opening in the roof to let in light. A shallow pool in the centre, beneath the opening, collected rain water. Guests were received in the atrium, which was also used for family gatherings.

FACT BOX

- The ancient Romans built aqueducts, or artificial channels, to transport water from mountain springs to the cities. It is believed that these channels provided about 1,928 litres of water per person each day! The aqueducts were usually supported by arches.

- The Column of Trajan houses a 200-step, spiral staircase that leads to the top. The carved marble monument once also housed a golden urn with the ashes of the Roman emperor Trajan.

- The Romans were very careful builders. In order to ensure that a wall was perfectly straight, they used a weight on a string (a plumb bob). This gave them a vertical line.

This instrument was used by Roman builders and architects

ARCHITECTURE AND MONUMENTS

 Why did Roman builders use chisels?

Roman builders used chisels for the woodwork in buildings. Roof frames in Roman houses were usually made of wood and shaped with iron chisels.

Which statue depicts the myth of the founding of ancient Rome?

It is believed that Rome was founded by the twin brothers Romulus and Remus, who were the sons of Mars, the Roman god of war. They were abandoned at birth and brought up by a she-wolf. A bronze statue of a she-wolf suckling two babies was made in honour of this belief.

 What events took place at the Circus Maximus?

The Circus Maximus was a huge stadium with an oval-shaped track where the popular Roman sport of chariot racing was held. The chariots were usually pulled by horses, though camels, dogs and even ostriches were used at times!

 What were Roman kitchens like?

In a Roman house, kitchens were usually quite small and tucked away in a corner. Many kitchens were probably dimly lit and not well ventilated.

 How did the Romans build their walls?

A Roman wall was usually made with bricks, stone and concrete. Two low walls of brick or stone were built with a gap in between, which was filled with concrete. After the concrete dried and hardened, more layers were added on top.

The Romans used bricks and concrete to make strong walls

MYTHOLOGY

The gods and goddesses of Roman mythology have a lot in common with those of Greek mythology. However, the Romans had different names for their deities.

Thunder and Lightning

The supreme Greek god, Zeus, is the Roman god Jupiter. Zeus's wife Hera is Juno, the wife of Jupiter. The attributes and symbols of many of the deites also remained the same - for example, Jupiter's thunderbolt and Mercury's winged shoes.

A Popular God

Apollo is one of the few gods who the Greeks and Romans called by the same name. The Roman emperor Augustus made Apollo his patron. During his reign a temple was built in honour of Apollo.

Personal Gods

The Romans worshiped some of their own gods too. There was the two-headed Janus. Each family also worshiped household gods called lares (or protective spirits) in a special shrine in the house.

The two-headed god Janus could look in opposite directions at the same time

MYTHOLOGY

 Which Roman god wears a blindfold?

Cupid, the Roman god of love, is often depicted as a little boy with wings and a blindfold. He is also portrayed as an adult, with the beautiful Psyche as his lover.

Cupid, the god of love, could not see who he was shooting with his arrow

 How was the Roman goddess Juno related to Jupiter?

Juno, the Roman goddess of marriage and childbirth, was Jupiter's sister as well as his wife!

 Which Roman god's symbol was the trident?

Neptune, the Roman god of the sea, carried a three-pronged spear, or a trident.

The blacksmith god Vulcan, who did his work beneath a volcano

 Who was the blacksmith among Roman gods?

Vulcan, the Roman god of fire, made weapons and armour for all the other gods. He was associated with volcanic eruptions. The word "volcano" is derived from his name.

 Who was the Roman goddess of dawn?

Aurora was the Roman goddess of dawn. The sun was her brother, and the moon, her sister.

Which Roman deity had the ass as her sacred animal?

The ass was the sacred animal of Vesta, the Roman goddess of the household. A flame was always kept burning in her temple.

Which creature is associated with the Roman god Faunus?

Faunus, the Roman god of woodlands, was often accompanied by half man, half goat creatures called fauns. During the Lupercalia festival held in his honour, priests (called "Luperci") walked the streets wearing goatskin and hit passers-by with belts made of goatskin.

A faun was an imaginary half man, half goat creature

FACT BOX

- Jupiter, the ruler of the Roman gods, is also known as Jove. He is the god of light and the sky.

- The Roman god Silvanus gets his name from the Latin word "silva", which means wood or forest. Silvanus was the guardian of forests and woodlands, as well as the protector of cattle.

- The Roman goddess Ceres always carried a bundle of the ears of corn because she was the goddess of agriculture. The word "cereal" comes from her name.

The bundle of corn was a symbol of prosperity and fertility

MYTHOLOGY

It is said that the hippocampus pulled the chariot of the sea god Neptune

 Was the hippocampus a fish or a horse?

In ancient Roman mythology, the hippocampus was a creature with the head and upper body of a horse, and the tail of a fish

Isis, the Egyptian goddess, was also worshiped in ancient Rome

 What did the Roman goddess Flora represent?

Flora was the Roman goddess of flowers. An ancient festival called the Floralia was held in her honour between April 28 and May 1.

 Which Egyptian goddess was also worshiped by the ancient Romans?

The popular Egyptian goddess Isis was also worshiped by the ancient Romans.

 Why does the Roman god Janus have two faces?

Janus was the Roman god of entrances. He was often portrayed with two heads to show that he had the ability to look in two directions at once.

 **What did the Roman goddess Luna represent?**

Luna, which means "moon" in Latin, was the Roman goddess of the moon. She was often shown riding through the sky in a white chariot.

LEGENDS AND HEROES

As the legend goes, Romulus and Remus decided to build a town but had an argument about who should be the king. So they agreed to wait for a good omen. Remus saw six vultures flying past and he thought it to be a sign in his favour. Soon after, however, Romulus saw 12! Eventually, Romulus killed Remus and founded the city of Rome on Palatine Hill.

Heroic Hercules

Many of the legends and heroes of Roman mythology are borrowed from the Greeks. The Roman mythological hero, Hercules, was inspired by a Greek heroic character, Heracles. In Roman legend, Hercules was the son of the god Jupiter, but his mother was an earthly being. His stepmother, the goddess Juno, was jealous of him and put two snakes in his cradle when he was a baby. However, the infant Hercules was so strong that he killed the snakes.

Hercules had superhuman strength even as a baby

Hercules was widely depicted in Roman sculptures and paintings. The Temple of Hercules was built in his honour.

LEGENDS AND HEROES

How did Horatius save Rome?

During a fierce battle against the Etruscans, the Roman hero Horatius defended the only remaining bridge leading into Rome. He stayed on the bridge and held back the enemy, while his fellow Romans cut the bridge. After the mission was completed, he dived into the Tiber River and swam back to Rome.

Who were the Furies?

The Furies were three sisters who represented revenge and lived in the underworld. They punished sinners and wicked people. Although the Furies were cruel, they were also believed to be just.

How was Cupid born?

According to some Roman legends, Cupid was born from a silver egg. The name Cupid has its root in the Latin word *cupidos*, which means "desire".

What kind of hair did Medusa have?

Medusa was a monster with living snakes as hair. She was first described in the ancient Greek myths, but later became a part of Roman legend as well. In Greek mythology, she was considered to be one of a group of three monstrous figures called Gorgons. Anything that Medusa looked at was believed to instantly turn into stone!

Horatius saved Rome from being conquered

26

A basilisk's eyes could turn a living creature to stone

 Which creature could kill with its eyes?

According to Greek and Roman legends, a deadly monster known as the basilisk could kill with one look from its eyes. This creature is also called a cockatrice because of the belief that it was hatched by either a snake or a toad from a cock's egg.

 Who was the Roman goddess Trivia?

Trivia was the Roman goddess of crossroads. Her name means "of the three ways". She is comparable to the Greek goddess Hecate, who haunted three-way junctions. Hecate was usually shown with three heads, each facing a different direction.

 What is the Roman name of the Greek hero Odysseus?

The Greek hero Odysseus, on whom the epic *Odyssey* (by the Greek poet Homer) is based, was known as Ulysses to the Romans. In one of his legendary adventures, Odysseus fights the six-headed monster Scylla.

A flock of geese raised an alarm and saved Rome

FACT BOX

■ The Roman hero Mucius is said to have deliberately burnt his right hand when he was captured by the Etruscan army. The Etruscan king was so impressed that he decided to release Mucius, who then got the name "Scaevola" (meaning "left-handed").

■ Ancient Roman legend has it that Venus, the Roman goddess of love and beauty, was born from the bubbles of the Mediterranean Sea.

■ It is believed that Rome was saved from an invasion because of the timely warning by a flock of geese kept in the shrine of Juno, a Roman goddess. A Roman general called Marcus Furius Camillus built a temple on Capitoline Hill in honour of this legend.

LEGENDS AND HEROES

 Who were the "Heavenly Twins"?

The two brothers Castor and Pollux (also called Polydeuces) were known as the "Heavenly Twins". They are associated with the star constellation Gemini. Two of the brightest stars in this constellation are named after the twins.

The Gemini constellation has two stars named after the twins Castor and Pollux

 Who is the hero in Virgil's epic, the *Aeneid*?

The hero of the *Aeneid* is Aeneas, the great mythological soldier of the Trojan War. The *Aeneid* was written by the Roman poet Virgil in praise of Aeneas, who was considered to be the symbol of an ideal Roman hero.

Who were the Centaurs?

In Roman mythology, the Centaurs were a legendary race of creatures that were half human and half horse. They had the faces of humans and the legs of horses!

Who was Dido?

Dido was the queen of the North African kingdom of Carthage. According to legend, the Trojan hero Aeneas and Dido fell in love with each other, but she killed herself when Aeneas was forced to leave her and sail away to Italy.

Dido, the Queen of Carthage, was heartbroken after Aeneas sailed away to Rome

Why is Arria regarded as a Roman heroine?

According to legend, Arria's husband was ordered by the Roman emperor Claudius to kill himself, but he could not bear to do it. Arria then took her husband's dagger, stabbed herself with it, and assured him that it did not hurt.

ARMY

The Roman army was a strong, well-organised force. It was the first full-time professional army in the world, comprising of soldiers for whom the army was a proper career and a means to earn wages. It was compulsory for soldiers to serve in the army for a minimum of 25 years!

Legions

The Roman army centred round its legions. The legion was subdivided into units called cohorts, and then into centuries.

Dagger

Infantry

The Roman legion prided itself on its well-trained infantry, or foot soldiers. A cavalry unit had about 500 soldiers on horseback.

Campaigns

The Roman wars were carefully planned campaigns. A camp commandant supervised the various units. A Roman army never retired for the night without digging trenches and putting up walls around its camp. Besides his weapons, each soldier carried his food provisions as well as kits for pitching camp.

Javelin

ARMY

 Which were the biggest units in the Roman army?

The legions were the biggest units in the Roman army. Each legion could have up to 6,000 soldiers.

 How did a Roman soldier protect himself in battle?

A Roman legionary carried a heavy shield called *scutum* to protect himself.

 Were Roman soldiers always on the move?

Roman soldiers had to march long distances - from one part of the vast Roman empire to another - in order to defend the land from attacks and invasions. They marched all day and rested at night.

This type of catapult could hurl big stones at enemy soldiers

 How did the ballista work?

The ballista was a catapult used by the Roman army during a siege of a city or fort. It could hurl heavy stones over walls.

Roman soldiers resting after a long day's march

What was the sacramentum?

When a Roman soldier enrolled in legionary service, he swore a solemn military oath (sacramentum) to the general and the emperor promising that he would fulfil his duties even to the point of death.

What would you find on top of a Roman soldier's helmet?

A Roman soldier's helmet had a ring or plume holder on top so that a plume could be fastened if necessary.

What was a cohort?

A cohort was a group of about 500 warriors. A cohort was further divided into a century, which was made up of 80 to 100 soldiers.

FACT BOX

■ Legend has it that Emperor Claudius II did not allow his soldiers to get married. A Roman priest, St Valentine, got many soldiers married secretly to protest against the rule. This is how Valentine's Day came about.

■ A group of 80 to 100 Roman soldiers was called a century. A centurion was the commanding officer of a century.

■ Ancient Roman soldiers cooked their meals in ovens built into the fort walls. The food was cooked in paterae, or mess tins. It is said that soldiers sometimes wore mess tins as helmets!

A soldier's cooking pan even doubled as a helmet at times!

ARMY

 What was the significance of a standard?

The standard was a tall pole crowned with various badges and symbols, including those of animals. Later, the image of the emperor also appeared in many standards. In the battlefield, the standards helped to keep the scattered units together.

A soldier in full gear

 How were Roman soldiers paid?

Salt as wages

Roman soldiers were often paid their salary in salt, which was a rare and precious commodity. The word "salary" can be traced to the Roman word for salt, *salarium*.

 **What were Roman shields made of?**

Roman shields were usually made from planks of wood and covered with leather.

 **How did the Romans arm themselves?**

A Roman soldier was armed with a short sword and a throwing spear called *pilum*. His protective covering included overlapping iron straps, a metal helmet and a rectangular shield that curved around his body.

How long did a Roman soldier's pair of boots last?

Roman soldiers are said to have needed at least a couple of pairs of boots every year. It has been estimated that a Roman soldier's boots would roughly last for about 483 kilometres (300 miles) of marching on our modern metalled roads.

WARS

Ancient Rome is remembered as one of the greatest military powers in history. To start with, though, it was only a tiny city-state that had to fight for its very existence against powerful neighbours. Gradually, the Romans built up a strong army that fought and won many wars.

The Etruscans

Among Rome's earliest foes were the Etruscans. The superior Etruscans, however, were unable to conquer Rome.

Punic Wars

The first Punic War was fought against the people of Carthage during 264-241 B.C. The object was to conquer Sicily.

In the second Punic War, the Carthaginian leader Hannibal took Rome by surprise by crossing the Alps. The Romans suffered their bloodiest defeat in the battle of Cannea.

Finally, the Roman commander Scipio Africanus took charge and led his army to victory in the Punic War.

Other important Roman battles included Trajan's campaigns against Dacia and the Battle of Cynoscephalae.

The mighty Roman sword conquered many lands

WARS

How was Britain conquered by the Romans?

Julius Caesar attacked Britain twice, in 54 B.C. and 55 B.C., but without success. Finally, in A.D. 43, Emperor Claudius sent a huge army that invaded Britain and conquered it.

Hannibal and his war elephants

What was the Pax Romana?

The Pax Romana, or "Roman Peace", refers to a time of harmony in the Roman Empire. Lasting over 200 years, it was a period of tremendous progress in Roman literature, arts and other creative activities.

Who was Pompey the Great?

The Roman general Pompey was a part of the First Triumvirate. It was a powerful group of three rulers that included Julius Caesar, Crassus and Pompey.

Spartacus fought against the mighty Roman army

Who was Spartacus?

Spartacus was a Roman slave who led a rebellion against the Roman Empire. He was killed in the battle that took place between the rebels and a huge Roman army.

Why did Hannibal cross the Alps?

Hannibal was a military general from Carthage who marched through the Alps mountains to fight the Romans. He was accompanied by a huge army of soldiers, cavalry and war elephants.

Why did Julius Caesar cross the Rubicon?

Julius Caesar defied Roman law to lead his army across the Rubicon River and conquer Gaul (the ancient name for France). Now we say "cross the Rubicon" when we refer to an important decision that cannot be reversed!

From which battle did Mark Antony and Cleopatra flee?

The Roman consul Mark Antony and his Egyptian queen, Cleopatra, fled from the Battle of Actium, which was fought against Octavian (Emperor Augustus, as he was known later).

FACT BOX

■ According to some historical accounts, the Roman emperor Constantine had a vision of Jesus Christ before he won the Battle of Milvian Bridge. After his victory he became a supporter of Christianity.

■ Roman commanding officers, such as centurions, wore a helmet topped with a crest. Soldiers could then easily spot their officer in the battlefield and follow him.

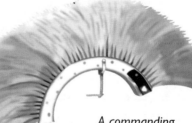

A commanding officer's crest

Visigoths, led by King Alaric, invaded Rome in A.D. 410 and plundered the city. In A.D. 455, Rome was again attacked and destroyed by a Germanic people called the Vandals.

WARS

 Who was Boudicca?

Boudicca was the queen of the Iceni tribe in East Anglia, England. In A.D. 61 she led her tribe in a revolt when the Romans increased the taxes. Boudicca and her army marched to Colchester and attacked the town, but the Romans soon defeated them. Rather than getting captured, Boudicca drank poison and died.

Statue of Boudicca, warrior queen of the Iceni tribe

 What was the most important standard of a Roman legion?

A Roman aquila (eagle) standard

To an ancient Roman soldier, the most important standard was the legionary eagle. Usually made of bronze or silver, it was a symbol of Rome's power and the legion's honour. It was considered shameful to lose it.

How did Horatius hold off the Etruscan army?

When the Etruscan army was on the verge of attacking Rome, Horatius prevented them from crossing a bridge into the city. He asked his fellow Romans to destroy the bridge while he held off the Etruscans.

Why was Carthage such an important state?

In the 3rd century B.C., Carthage was the greatest naval power of the Mediterranean region. It controlled the flow of trade in the Mediterranean and became very rich from the gold and silver mines of Spain. It expanded over most of North Africa at the time of the Roman conquest of the Peninsula of Italy.

What was the tortoise formation?

Legionaries arranged themselves in special formations in the battlefield. Faced with the enemy's arrows and spears, the legionaries protected their bodies and heads with their shields, getting into what was called the tortoise formation.

ACHIEVEMENTS

The Etruscans, who reigned in Rome for nearly a century, left behind a rich legacy. This included the city's first ramparts and a sewage drainage system called the Cloaca Maxima. In time, a large network of roads connected most corners of the empire. This, in turn, enhanced trade and commerce. Literary and artistic activities flourished too.

Latin, the language of the ancient Romans, forms the basis of many modern European languages. We still use Roman numerals, especially in watches and clocks.

A modern clock with Roman numerals

Central Heating

The inventive Romans constructed rooms on top of stones so that hot air from furnaces could flow in the space between the ground and the building. The heated air thus warmed the entire building. This early type of central heating was called hypocaust.

Water Wheel

The Romans invented water wheels to pump water out of mines. Other astonishing inventions by these creative people included straight roads, flushing lavatories, hamburgers and makeup!

ACHIEVEMENTS

 How many continents was the Roman Empire spread across?

At its height, the Roman Empire was spread over parts of Europe, Africa and Asia.

 How were the Romans associated with the city of London?

In the 1st century A.D., the Romans established Londinium to the north of the Thames valley. This settlement later became the city of London.

 How vast was the network of Roman roads?

The Roman Empire, stretching from Mesopotamia in Asia to Britain, had a huge network of roads, adding up to over 80,500 kilometres (50,000 miles). A few ancient Roman roads are in use even today.

 Which languages can be traced to the ancient Romans?

Several European languages - such as Italian, French and Spanish - developed from Latin, which was the language of the Roman Empire.

 Why do many towns and cities in Britain owe their names to the Romans?

The names of towns ending in "chester", "caster", or "cester" can be traced back to the ancient Roman period. The Latin word for "camp" is "castra" and hence, there were such names as Dorchester, Doncaster and Cirencester - which were Roman camps at one time.

Roman travellers crossing one of the many bridges that connected the network of roads in ancient Rome

Did a Roman slave write timeless fables?

An ancient Roman writer named Phaedrus, who was born a slave, rewrote many fables attributed to the legendary Aesop. Phaedrus's stories - such as *The Fox and the Sour Grapes* and *The Wolf and the Lamb* - survive to this day.

The fox could not reach the grapes in the fable of "The Fox and the Sour Grapes"

Why is the modern-day census attributed to Rome?

The modern idea of a state counting the population is a direct legacy from the Romans. The word "census" itself is Latin. The Roman census process involved a sworn declaration of age, family and property.

FACT BOX

■ The Roman emperor Justinian created the Justinian Code, which is a collection of all the ancient Roman laws. It is the basis of all the justice systems of the modern western world.

■ In A.D. 313, the Roman emperor Constantine issued the Edict of Milan. This made Christianity a legal religion. In A.D. 380, Emperor Theodosius the Great gave it the status of official religion.

■ Roman engineers were among the best in the world. They built roads, bridges, aqueducts and long networks of drains and sewers. They used instruments such as folding foot rules, dividers and plumb bobs (bronze weights) to make precise calculations.

Roman engineering instruments were very advanced

ACHIEVEMENTS

How long did the Roman Empire last?

The Romans first came to power about 200 B.C. By A.D. 100, they ruled a vast empire. The empire started collapsing in the 5th century A.D., after the city of Rome was attacked by warrior tribes.

Did the ancient Romans actually invent concrete?

Long-lasting concrete for building was first developed by the ancient Romans.

Who conquered Gaul?

Gaul (modern France) was conquered by the Roman leader Julius Caesar.

Which was the first government to introduce a public health programme?

The ancient Romans did a lot to improve their public health system. In this sense, theirs was the first civilisation to introduce a programme of public health for everyone. Doctors used medical instruments like probes, folding knives, scalpels and forceps to operate on patients.

Surgical hooks

Spatula

Probe

What was unique about Santa Sophia?

Built by Emperor Justinian, Santa Sophia was the biggest church of its time. The building still exists in Istanbul, and is now called the Hagia Sophia or Aya Sophia.

Santa Sophia was the largest church of its time

UNUSUAL FACTS

The ninth, tenth, eleventh and twelfth months in our calendar come from Latin words that mean seventh, eighth, ninth and tenth!

A Numbers Game

Our modern calendar was established by the ancient Romans. It had 10 months then - from March to December. December was named after the Latin word for tenth, November for ninth, and so on. When January and February were added later, September became the ninth month, though its old meaning remained!

Naming of the Months

January, February and March are respectively named after the gods Janus, Februus and Mars. May and June probably take their names from the goddesses Maia and Juno. July and August are named after the Roman leaders Julius Caesar and Augustus Caesar.

Julius Caesar - after whom the month of July is named

UNUSUAL FACTS

The volcano Mount Vesuvius erupted very suddenly

What remained buried under ash for hundreds of years?

In A.D. 79, the volcano Mount Vesuvius erupted without any warning. The people of Pompeii, a Roman town at the foot of the volcano, tried to escape, but many got buried alive under layers of hot ash and burning cinders. Pompeii remained buried under volcanic ash until it was discovered by archaeologists in the 18th century.

Did books exist before the time of the ancient Romans?

The ancient Romans were the first to create books in the shape that we now have. Earlier, people used scrolls of parchment or papyrus. The Romans joined sheets of parchment to make books with pages that could be turned.

Did ancient Romans eat with their hands?

Ancient Romans ate either with their fingers or with spoons. They did not use table knives and forks.

Spoon

What were the Saxon Shore forts?

The Saxon Shore forts were built by the Romans on the southeast coast of England. These were meant to protect the Roman Empire against attacks from across the English Channel and North Sea.

What did Roman brides wear around their waist?

Roman brides wore an orange veil and a belt with a special knot

Ancient Roman brides wore a belt tied in a knot around their waist. This could be untied only by the groom. The knot was called the Knot of Hercules because Roman mythology regarded Hercules as the guardian of married life.

Why did ancient Romans wear engagement rings on the forth finger of the left hand?

Ancient Romans wore engagement rings on the forth finger of the left hand because they believed that this finger was directly connected by a nerve to the heart.

Who was the African emperor of ancient Rome?

Septimius Severus, an African from Libya, was the Roman emperor from A.D. 193 to 211.

FACT BOX

■ It is believed that there were female gladiators in ancient Rome. Archaeologists have found the remains of a girl who might have been a gladiator. A carving of two female combatants has also been found.

■ In ancient Rome people called "fullers" cleaned clothes by rubbing urine on dirty clothes and brushing them with combs!

■ Roman students carried candles with them since the school day began well before sunrise, when it was still dark.

A Roman school child had to carry a candle to school

43

UNUSUAL FACTS

A coin was placed on a dead person's mouth

 What did the goddess Cloacina look after?

The Romans were very particular about their drains and sewers, and they even had a special goddess, named Cloacina, who was in charge of their drainage systems. Her name was connected to the Roman word *cloaca*, which means "drain".

 Why was a new-born baby placed at its father's feet?

A Roman father had complete authority over his child's life. If he picked up the child placed at his feet, it showed that he had accepted the child. However, if the father ignored the baby, then it was either doomed to die or could be taken away by someone else.

 Why did Roman people put a coin on a dead person's mouth?

The ancient Romans believed that when a person died his or her spirit went to the underworld. The spirit could reach the underworld only by crossing a river called Styx. The coin was given as a payment for Charon, the ferryman of the underworld.

 Did Roman schoolchildren get a midday break?

In ancient Roman schools, children got a midday break for lunch and a nap. They went back to school around mid-afternoon to complete their studies.

Did the Romans bury their dead in underground chambers?

In ancient Rome there were underground burial chambers with rooms and corridors. These were known as catacombs. Graves were cut into the walls of the catacombs and sealed with bricks or marble.

Catacombs were of a network of underground burial chambers